CHRIST

in Every Book *of the* Bible

by Oral Roberts

Revised Edition

Unless otherwise indicated,
all Scripture quotations are from the
King James Version of the Bible.

RICHARD
ROBERTS
ORAL ROBERTS MINISTRIES

Contents

Introduction

CHRIST IS THE heart and central theme of the Bible. From Genesis to Revelation, the message revolves around the person and work of Jesus Christ. All things reveal Him and point to Him.

When God spoke the world into existence, Jesus Christ was there. From before creation Christ was, and into the eternal ages He is. He is the same yesterday, today, and forever. The Scripture declares, "In the beginning was the Word, and the Word was with God, and the Word was God. And the Word was made flesh, and dwelt among us" *(John 1:1,14).*

Jesus said, "I am Alpha and Omega, the beginning and the ending" *(Revelation 1:8).* The alphabet is the cornerstone of all literature. The numberless volumes in the libraries of the world are composed of a varying combination of its twenty-six letters. *Alpha* is the first word in the Greek alphabet and *omega* is the last. Jesus chose these two symbols to describe Himself. Had He been speaking in English, He would have said, "I am the A and the Z." Or, "I am the alphabet."

What the alphabet is to literature, Christ is to all of life. He is its essence, its structure, and its composition. Jesus is called the Word of God because He is the full thought or expression of the mind of God. We know and understand the Father through Christ. He conveys the truth of God to us just as the alphabet is the vehicle for bringing the thought of the author to the mind of the reader.

As we read the Bible, it invites us to see that Christ permeates the Word of God with His presence, and as He springs forth from every page, it is to meet every man in the form of his need. The Word says He knows our life from A to Z. He is acquainted with all our ways, and He is touched with the feelings of our infirmities. Such a Savior is sufficient to meet all our needs.

As I behold the wonders of Christ in God's Word, the sheer beauty and harmony of the Man fills my eyes with tears and I cry, "O Lord, that I might be like You!" I pray this will be your feeling also as you read this book and become acquainted with Him through His Word.

Your partner,

Oral Roberts

In GENESIS…
He Is the Seed of the Woman

FROM THE BEGINNING, there was an intimacy and warmth between God and man. Hebrew history has Adam saying to all creation: "Come, and let us go…and accept the kingship of Him who created us." Joy and gladness spread throughout the earth, and all creatures of God began to shout, "Hello, God!" And God, looking upon His masterpiece—the crown of His creation—warmly embraced him and said, "Hello, Man!" It was a celebration of life!

When Adam and Eve chose to eat of the tree of knowledge of good and evil, in that moment something inside them died. They didn't feel comfortable with God anymore. They cried, "Let's run and hide." For the first time, man was afraid, for he recognized his vulnerability—his mortality. Man, through using his power of choice irresponsibly and saying yes to the devil and no to God, lost his being as a whole man.

This is what we call "the fall of man." And it resulted in the awful fears and the alienation from God that man feels today. But even in the midst of man's rebellion, God's love held strong! God said to the devil, "I will put enmity between thee and the woman, and between thy seed and her seed; it shall bruise thy head, and thou shalt bruise his heel" *(Genesis 3:15)*.

Here is the first promise of Jesus Christ, our Redeemer. This is perhaps the *seed* Scripture of the entire Bible. The *seed of the woman* refers to the miraculous virgin birth of Christ and speaks of the outer humanity of Jesus. The Bible message is positive. From the first day of sin, God in His great love proclaimed a plan for our salvation. He promised a Savior.

God was saying to the devil, "You and man will be in conflict. There will always be this conflict of interest, this division between you. And you will bruise or injure the humanity of Jesus," which refers to Jesus being nailed to the cross. But God says, in essence: "Devil, you are a defeated foe. The Redeemer will crush your head—your brain and mind and spirit. Everything that comprises your knowing will be destroyed. The Seed of the woman will smash your head."

This is in harmony with the Scripture where our Lord said, "Be of good cheer; I have overcome the world" *(John 16:33)*. And 1 John 3:8, "For this purpose the Son of God was manifested, that he might destroy the works of the devil."

God's plan of redemption was completed when Jesus bowed His head on Calvary and said, "It is finished" *(John 19:30)*. How Satan's head must have been bruised when the followers of Jesus went to the sepulcher and found that He had risen!

The final bruising of the serpent's head will come when Satan and his evil offspring are cast into the lake of fire forever and ever.

In EXODUS...
He Is the Passover Lamb

THE PASSOVER BEAUTIFULLY represents the Atonement—At-one-ment! This means that through the blood of Jesus Christ, the sinner and God are made one.

God instituted the Passover so that the first-born of the Israelites might be saved from the great death that went through all the land of Egypt, and to commemorate their deliverance from Egypt's bondage and affliction. God told Moses and Aaron to tell the people to slay a lamb without blemish and to take a branch of hyssop and splash the blood of the lamb on the sides and tops of the doors of their houses. "For the Lord will pass through to smite the Egyptians; and when he seeth the blood…the Lord will pass over the door, and will not suffer the destroyer to come in unto your houses to smite you" *(Exodus 12:23).* This is a picture of the cross. Israel followed the plan of the Lord, and they were saved from the great death.

The lamb of the Passover was a type of Jesus Christ, the Lamb of God. When John the Baptist saw Jesus coming to him, he said, "Behold the Lamb of God, which taketh away the sin of the world" *(John 1:29).* Paul declared, "Christ our passover is sacrificed for us" *(1 Corinthians 5:7).*

Today we are saved not by the blood of animals, but by the precious blood of Jesus Christ, our Passover Lamb, who is "without blemish and without spot" *(1 Peter 1:19)*.

The thrust of Jesus' whole life was to go to the cross. Think of any human need or feeling—any sin, any hurt, sickness, fear, loneliness, despair, or suffering—and realize that Jesus gathered these up and carried them with Him to the cross, and He bore them there in His own body vicariously for us *(Isaiah 53:5)*. The old rugged cross is not just two pieces of wood. It is the stretched out, bleeding form of Jesus Christ our Passover Lamb, who took all of our needs and carried them in His own body.

His blood applied to our hearts through faith gives us protection from the destruction of our archenemy Satan.

In LEVITICUS...
He Is Our High Priest

ONCE A YEAR, on the Great Day of Atonement, the Israelites brought sacrifices of goats and bullocks to the tabernacle of the Lord to atone for their sins. After the high priest had offered a sin offering for himself and his family, he killed an animal and burned it on the altar for the people. Then, with some of the blood of the slain sacrifice, he again entered the Holy of Holies and sprinkled the blood on the Ark of the Covenant. Thus he asked God to receive the blood and the offering as an atonement for the sins of the people *(Leviticus 16:11–16)*.

This is a picture of Christ's entrance into heaven to present before the Father His atoning blood for our sins and transgressions. The Levitical high priests offered sacrifices that made nothing perfect. They only temporarily covered the people's sins and had to be repeated every year. "But Christ being come an high priest of good things to come, by a greater and more perfect tabernacle, not made with hands… neither by the blood of goats and calves, but by his own blood he entered in once into the holy place, having obtained *eternal redemption* for us" *(Hebrews 9:11–12)*.

Think of it! Eternal redemption. The new covenant was made. "This is the covenant that I will make with them after those days, saith the Lord, I will put my laws into their hearts, and in their minds will I write them; and their sins and iniquities will I remember no more" *(Hebrews 10:16–17).*

The Levitical high priests died. But Jesus Christ, "because he continueth ever, hath an unchangeable priesthood. Wherefore he is able also to save them to the uttermost that come unto God by him, seeing *he ever liveth* to make intercession for them" *(Hebrews 7:24–25).*

One of the most important qualities of our High Priest, Jesus Christ, is that He is "touched with the feeling of our infirmities"—our problems and needs *(Hebrews 4:15).* He knows the feelings we experience because He was tempted in all points like we are "yet without sin." Therefore, God says that we can "come boldly unto the throne of grace, that we may obtain mercy, and find grace to help in time of need" *(Hebrews 4:16).*

How difficult it may be to remember when some problem is tearing you up inside. But it is true. Jesus Christ is always at the point of your need. Wherever you are and whatever condition you are in, God desires to be alive and active in your life!

In NUMBERS...
He Is the Pillar of Cloud by Day and the Pillar of Fire by Night

"AND ON THE DAY that the tabernacle was reared up the cloud covered the tabernacle, namely, the tent of the testimony: and at even there was upon the tabernacle as it were the appearance of fire, until the morning. So it was alway: the cloud covered it by day, and the appearance of fire by night" *(Numbers 9:15–16).*

When the children of Israel made their journey toward the Promised Land, "the Lord went before them by day in a pillar of a cloud, to lead them the way; and by night in a pillar of fire, to give them light; to go by day and night" *(Exodus 13:21).*

The Scripture tells us that when the cloud moved, the people moved and followed. When the cloud stopped, they stopped and rested, no matter how long it was—"whether it were two days, or a month, or a year" *(Numbers 9:22).*

What a magnificent illustration of God's faithfulness to guide His people when they are willing and obedient!

Jesus Christ is our Pillar of Cloud and Pillar of Fire—our Guide. He said, "I am the way," and, "He that followeth me shall not walk in darkness, but shall have the light of life" *(John 14:6; 8:12)*.

The promise that God will guide those who seek Him is clearly set forth in the total sweep of the Bible *(Isaiah 30:21)*. What can a Christian do without God's guidance? This life is a series of paths...some broad, some narrow. We often come to forks where the road ends, and we are in a dilemma as to which way to take. When we cannot see into the future, how important it is that we have a guide who sees all things and knows all things. Jesus Christ leads us in the right paths as we follow Him *(Psalm 23:3)*.

In DEUTERONOMY... He Is the Prophet Like unto Moses

GOD TOLD MOSES, "I will raise them up a Prophet from among their brethren, like unto thee, and will put my words in his mouth; and he shall speak unto them all that I shall command him" *(Deuteronomy 18:18).*

God fulfilled this promise. Philip said of Jesus, "We have found him, of whom Moses in the law, and the prophets, did write, Jesus of Nazareth" *(John 1:45).*

In all His lifetime, Christ never lost sight of His relationship with His Father. "I am in the Father, and the Father in me," He said. It was a consciousness of this relationship with God that made Jesus the irresistible force that He was on earth. When He stretched out His hand to touch the afflicted, the blind, the maimed, the deaf, He radiated His faith that the Father's hand was in His hand. Christ never doubted, never feared. In meeting the crises of life, His attitude was, "I speak and My Father speaks with Me. I and My Father are one." *(Read John 5:19,43; 8:28; 10:25.)*

In so many ways, Moses and Jesus were alike. "Moses was very meek, above all the men which were upon the face of the earth" *(Numbers 12:3).*

Jesus said, "I am meek and lowly in heart" *(Matthew 11:29)*.

Meekness is not weakness as some people believe, but an attribute of spiritual strength. Neither is it being a dishrag or something for people to tread upon. Meekness is dynamic, positive action. Meekness *closes* a mouth in time of temper. It *forgives* an insult. Meekness is *submission* to God, so that He can do His mighty works through you. Moses—who courageously delivered the judgments of God to the mighty Egyptian Pharaoh...who led the Israelites 40 years in the wilderness...and who spoke with God face-to-face—was anything but a weakling. And certainly there was nothing weak about Jesus. His strong faith and His perfect contact with heaven filled His entire being with power.

Moses delivered the Israelites out of Egyptian bondage. Jesus is the promised Deliverer. He came "to preach deliverance to the captives [people in bondage], and recovering of sight to the blind, to set at liberty them that are bruised" *(Luke 4:18)*.

Moses saw God work many miracles by his hand. Yet in far greater measure Jesus wrought miracle after miracle. He "went about doing good, and healing all that were oppressed of the devil; for God was with him" *(Acts 10:38).*

In JOSHUA...
He Is the Captain of Our Salvation

AFTER MOSES DIED, Joshua became the leader of Israel. He faced one of the greatest tasks of his life—the conquest of Jericho. This was a time of great stress for Joshua, and he needed help badly.

"When Joshua was by Jericho...he lifted up his eyes and looked, and, behold, there stood a man over against him with his sword drawn in his hand: and Joshua went unto him, and said unto him, Art thou for us, or for our adversaries? And he said, Nay; but as captain of the host of the Lord am I now come. And Joshua fell on his face to the earth, and did worship" *(Joshua 5:13–14).*

Joshua was made to know that the Captain of a mightier host than his was with him, the sword of whose strength was drawn and ready for the fight. With the Captain of the Lord's host, Joshua led the people to victory.

Jesus Christ is referred to as "the captain of *[our]* salvation" *(Hebrews 2:10).* A captain is a leader or originator (author), one who initiates and carries through. We are told to "run with patience the race that is set before us, looking unto Jesus the author and finisher of our faith" *(Hebrews 12:1–2).* Our faith is centered in Christ. It comes from Him, and He is the finisher and completer of it.

Jesus said, "Lo, I am with you alway, even unto the end of the world" *(Matthew 28:20).* He leads His heavenly host to do battle in the great conflicts of life. If our eyes were opened as were the eyes of Elisha's servant, we could see that we are not so much alone as we sometimes suppose we are *(2 Kings 6:16–17).*

Young David shouted to the giant who defied the armies of God: *The battle is the Lord's and He will give this enemy into my hands. (Read 1 Samuel 17:31–50.)* What is your battle? Perhaps it's a desire for vengeance. Lust. Alcoholism. An uncontrolled temper. A backbiting spirit.

Or some disease that's threatening your body. Whatever your enemy, it is not just coming against you personally; it's also challenging you as a creation of Almighty God. So in fighting the spiritual battle we can call on the Lord, the Captain of our Salvation, Jesus Christ, who is with us. When we recognize this, it can be the beginning of a new life for us.

In JUDGES...
He Is Our Judge and Lawgiver

TWO THINGS STAND out in the Book of Judges—the utter failure of Israel and the persistent grace of God to deliver them. Following the death of Joshua, "the Lord raised up judges, which delivered them out of the hand of those that spoiled them" *(Judges 2:16)*.

A judge is one who is invested with authority to determine litigated questions and one who gives a judgment. Christ, our Judge and Lawgiver, has all authority: He said, "All power is given unto me in heaven and in earth" *(Matthew 28:18)*.

It was Christ's method to hold out to people the good news of the Gospel—to show them a better life—but if it was rejected, then He told the truth about the consequences of sin. He taught that all sin will be punished unless it is repented of and forgiven by God. The lines are drawn for this, not only in the published laws of the Bible but also in the moral and physical laws of the universe.

One can know the punishment of sin by simply looking at the laws of nature, because all natural laws are based upon the spiritual laws in the Word of God. Jesus said, "Give, and it shall be given unto you…for with the same measure that ye mete withal it shall be measured to you again" *(Luke 6:38)*. He was saying that whatsoever you sow—good or bad—will be multiplied back to you *(Galatians 6:7–8)*.

When you make God your Source and sow good seed, you can expect to reap God's goodness and mercy. This is an infallible law. On the other hand, the seeds of sin work the same.

The judge is now our Savior Jesus Christ. He said, "If any man hear my words, and believe not, I judge him not: for I came not to judge the world, but *to save the world*. He that rejecteth me, and receiveth not my words, hath one that judgeth him: the word that I have spoken, the same shall judge him in the last day" *(John 12:47–48)*.

Christ's words *judge* us...but His life *saves* us. In 1 Timothy 1:15 the Apostle Paul said, "This is a faithful saying, and worthy of all acceptation, that Christ Jesus came into the world to save sinners; of whom I am chief." There is only one who can free us from the law of sin. That's our Lord Jesus Christ...our Judge and Lawgiver *(Romans 3:19–26)*. Not only can we have our sins forgiven today, but also our nature to sin can be changed now and forever!

In RUTH...
He Is Our Kinsman-Redeemer

THE BEAUTIFUL LOVE STORY of Ruth and Boaz gives an impressive type of Jesus Christ, our Kinsman-Redeemer.

Ruth and her mother-in-law, Naomi, returned to their homeland as widows and destitute. Ruth met Boaz, a kinsman of her deceased husband, and they fell in love and made plans to marry. According to Jewish custom, a kinsman had two duties. He was expected to marry the widow of the deceased and raise up seed unto the deceased, and it was his duty and privilege to purchase any inheritance in danger of lapsing or to redeem a lapsed one. However, he had to be willing to perform this duty and able to do so.

Boaz redeemed the land of Ruth and Naomi. He met all the requirements. He was a *kinsman,* he was *willing* to redeem the property, and he was *able* to redeem it. Of course Boaz was overjoyed to marry Ruth. He was in love with her.

When our Lord Jesus Christ entered the earth, He became one of us—bone of our bone, flesh of our flesh. This gave Him connection with man. Therefore, He is our *kinsman.* However, Christ's Spirit was not born of man, but of the Holy Spirit. This gave Him His connection with God.

Jesus *willingly* left heaven and its glories and came to earth to die on the cross for our redemption from the bondage of sin. The Bible says, "In his love and in his pity he redeemed them"

(Isaiah 63:9). Because of love, He was willing to become the ransom price to buy us back into the liberty of the sons of God.

Jesus Christ was the only one who was *able* to redeem us. None other could qualify.

In John's Revelation, he tells of seeing a book that was sealed with seven seals. But no one was able to open the book until the Lamb, Jesus Christ, who had been slain and raised from the dead, stepped forth and took the book out of the right hand of Him that sat upon the throne.

When He took the book, "the four beasts and four and twenty elders fell down before the Lamb... And they sung a new song, saying, Thou art worthy to take the book, and to open the seals thereof: for thou wast slain, and hast redeemed us to God by thy blood out of every kindred, and tongue...and nation" *(Revelation 5:8–9)*.

In 1 & 2 SAMUEL...
He Is Our Trusted Prophet

AT THE TIME THAT Eli was the judge and high priest over Israel, Samuel was just a little boy.

His mother dedicated him to the Lord, and she brought him to live with Eli and serve under his direction in the temple.

God was very displeased with Eli and his sons, for Eli had not trained his sons to be obedient, and they did wicked things in God's sight. The Lord told Eli, "I will raise me up a faithful priest, that shall do according to that which is in mine heart and in my mind: and I will build him a sure house; and he shall walk before mine anointed for ever" *(1 Samuel 2:35).*

God chose little Samuel to be the faithful and trusted priest and prophet to take Eli's place. Samuel grew, and the Lord was with him. He was faithful to do that which God directed him to do. He "did let none of his words fall to the ground" *(1 Samuel 3:19).*

Samuel was reliable, truthful, upright, steadfast, faithful, and trustworthy—dedicated to doing the will of God. Jesus Christ, our Trusted Prophet, has these same attributes.

If there is any one thing that stands out in the life of Jesus Christ, it is that He was completely dedicated to doing the will of His Heavenly Father.

Jesus lived His entire life to the end that He might bring glory to God and please Him. From a boy 12 years old—when His parents found Him in the temple and He said, "I must be about my Father's business," to the garden when He prayed, "Not my will, but thine be done"—His life existed solely to do the will of God *(Luke 2:49; 22:42)*.

By His very works, Jesus showed us that He is One on whom we can depend...One in whom we can fully trust.

In KINGS and CHRONICLES... He Is Our Reigning King

GOD PROMISED THAT the Messiah or Reigning King, Jesus Christ, would come through the lineage of David. The Lord told Solomon, "I will establish the throne of thy kingdom upon Israel for ever, as I promised to David thy father, saying, There shall not fail thee a man upon the throne of Israel" *(1 Kings 9:5). (Also see Genesis 22:15–18.)*

When the angel came to Mary, he said, "Behold, thou shalt conceive in thy womb, and bring forth a son, and shalt call his name JESUS. He shall be great, and shall be called the Son of the Highest: and the Lord God shall give unto him the throne of his father David: and he shall reign over the house of Jacob for ever; and of his kingdom there shall be no end" *(Luke 1:31–33)*.

The people were expecting the promised King to set up a literal kingdom. They looked for a king who would set them free from Roman rule and heavy taxation and who would set up his own rule here on earth.

When John the Baptist came out of the wilderness preaching, "The kingdom of heaven is at hand" *(Matthew 3:2),* he bore witness of Jesus Christ, whose kingdom was to be established in the hearts of men.

Jesus did not come riding on a white horse, waving a sword. Rather, He was born in a stable and laid in a lowly manger. Even when His followers recognized Him as the Lord of lords and King of kings, He rode a humble donkey into Jerusalem while they threw palm branches into His path and sang hosannas unto Him.

Christ's kingdom is one of the Spirit...one of power, love, and faith—a spiritual kingdom that is

entered by faith. Today Jesus Christ reigns in the
hearts of those who accept Him as their Lord and
Reigning King. In the end time, the kingdoms
of this world will literally "become the kingdoms
of our Lord, and of his Christ; and he shall reign
for ever and ever" *(Revelation 11:15)*. Then we
who have been faithful shall also reign with Him
throughout eternity.

In EZRA...
He Is Our Faithful Scribe

EZRA WAS THE SCRIBE who kept the official
records of the Jewish nation. He revered the Word
of the Lord. The Bible says he "prepared his heart
to seek the law of the Lord, and to do it, and to
teach in Israel statutes and judgments" *(Ezra 7:10)*.

After coming out of captivity, the people were
so hungry to hear the Word that Ezra read to
them from the Book of the Law from morning
to midday. So sweet and wonderful were the
words that "all the people wept when they heard
the words of the law" *(Nehemiah 8:9)*. And they
worshipped God out of their hearts.

In Ezra, we see Jesus as the Faithful Scribe who "went about all Galilee, teaching in their synagogues, and preaching the gospel of the kingdom, and healing all manner of sickness and all manner of disease among the people" *(Matthew 4:23).*

Christ's Sermon on the Mount still shows the way for us to live with our neighbors in harmony and peace. His parables teach their subtle stories of the secrets of life. His teachings about doers and hearers, givers and receivers, participants and spectators are unparalleled. Jesus teaches us how to live. "Fear not," He challenged; "believe only" and "All things are possible to him that believeth" *(Luke 8:50; Mark 9:23).*

He taught us to search the Scriptures, for in them we have eternal life. "And," He said, "they are they which testify of me" *(John 5:39).*

I used to watch my father read the Bible. He loved to sit in a chair leaning against the house in the cool of the day and read for hours. Frequently pausing to mark a passage, he would become so absorbed that he would be completely oblivious to his surroundings. We children could run and play and shout, but he would not be disturbed.

Sometimes he would look up, and I would see tears in his eyes. "Papa, why do you cry when you read the Bible?" I would ask.

Brushing the tears away and closing his Bible, he would smile and say, "Son, someday when the Lord Jesus is real to you as a person, when you feel Him standing by your side, when you know He is closer to you than your breath, then you will know and understand."

In the years that followed, I learned what Papa meant. When I accepted Christ into my heart I did not just embrace a great spirit, an idea, or a concept. I embraced a Person—Jesus Christ. Jesus is more than a Savior. To me, He is a friend and daily companion. We cannot go back 2,000 years ago with our needs. We bring Jesus into the NOW through the Bible. Through God's Word, He is here.

In NEHEMIAH...
He Is the Rebuilder of Broken Walls of Our Shattered Lives

WHEN NEHEMIAH HEARD about the broken-down walls of Jerusalem and the city lying waste, it grieved him tremendously. This was the city of his fathers. He was so burdened over the reproach the situation was bringing on God's people that he wept, fasted, and prayed to the extent he became almost physically ill.

Nehemiah was the king's cupbearer and was in the king's presence often. Seeing Nehemiah so sad, the king became quite concerned. Their conversation is recorded: "Then the king said unto me, For what dost thou make request? So I prayed to the God of heaven. And I said unto the king...send me unto Judah, unto the city...that I may build it" *(Nehemiah 2:4–5).*

There is no break in the continuity of the story. Nehemiah's prayer was an attitude toward God—a beautiful, almost unconscious habit of an uplifted heart. Needless to say, his prayer was answered. Because of the burden of his heart and his vision, he rebuilt the walls of Jerusalem in spite of ridicule, discouragements, and opposition.

Jesus specializes in rebuilding the broken walls of our shattered lives. He said that the Father sent Him "to heal the brokenhearted" *(Luke 4:18).*

This means that some people are bruised, fragmented, broken. Some people's personalities have been divided and are not whole. We can be tortured by fear on the one hand and inspired by great faith on the other. Sometimes fear overcomes faith, and sometimes faith overcomes fear. Seldom do some people go through a day when they are not broken, either in themselves or in some member of their family or neighbor. So Jesus is saying, "God has sent Me to heal you."

Jesus is the Mender of broken hearts, broken bodies, broken homes. No case is hopeless with Jesus Christ, the Rebuilder of Broken Walls.

In ESTHER...
He Is Our Mordecai

MORDECAI REFUSED TO bow and give reverence to Haman, a proud and wicked man. Angered, Haman used his influence with the king to send out a decree to put to death all the Jewish people of that nation, thus getting rid of Mordecai and his people.

When Mordecai heard this, he "rent his clothes, and put on sackcloth with ashes, and went out into the midst of the city, and cried with a loud and a bitter cry" *(Esther 4:1)*.

Mordecai revealed Haman's vile plot to the king through Queen Esther. Providentially, Haman died on his own gallows which he had prepared for Mordecai, and Mordecai was exalted to the second place in the kingdom.

Mordecai was not thinking so much of himself as of his people when he mourned and fasted for their deliverance. His was the sorrow of a godly man moved with compassion. His compassion moved him into the dynamic action which saved his people.

Christ has unparalleled compassion. It is written, "And Jesus went forth, and saw a great multitude, and was moved with compassion toward them, and he healed their sick" *(Matthew 14:14)*.

Now compassion is different from sympathy. *Sympathy* causes you to feel sorry for someone and say, "I wish I could do something for you." But it has little power to help anybody. *Compassion* is what Jesus felt when He healed the sick. It moves you to action.

Christ was so full of compassion for the suffering and the needs of others that He felt He must take their place, that He must deliver them. Matthew 8:17 says Christ "himself took our infirmities, and bare our sicknesses." He took them! *Willingly!* Christ, who had never been weak or sick, took our infirmities and our sicknesses upon His strong, healthy body. He also took our sins. God "made him to be sin for us, who knew no sin; that we might be made the righteousness of God in him" *(2 Corinthians 5:21).*

Such compassion is God's love in action. Jesus Christ is our compassionate Lord, our Mordecai!

In JOB...
He Is Our Ever-Living Redeemer

SINCE THE DAWN of time, one of the most important questions confronting man has been, does life continue after death?

In the abyss of Job's affliction, loss, and ridicule, he uttered words that thrill us to the very depth of our being: "I know that my redeemer liveth, and that he shall stand at the latter day upon the earth: and though after my skin worms destroy this body, yet in my flesh shall I see God: whom I shall see for myself, and mine eyes shall behold, and not another" *(Job 19:25–27)*.

Job looked through the eyes of faith and saw his own resurrection and an Ever-living Redeemer.

In John 11:25–26, Jesus said, "I am the resurrection, and the life: he that believeth in me, though he were dead, yet shall he live: and whosoever liveth and believeth in me shall never die."

Like Job, the Apostle Paul also knew that there is a hope beyond this life. He said, "If in this life only we have hope in Christ, we are of all men most miserable. But now is Christ risen from the dead" *(1 Corinthians 15:19–20)*.

The resurrection of Christ from the dead is seen as the greatest miracle of all time. But it is only a fact of history unless we take hold of its power for our everyday lives. Jesus said, "Because I live, ye shall live also" *(John 14:19)*. He meant this to apply to newness of life in living as well as to our final victory over the grave.

The Resurrection is more than resurrection of the body at the end time. The Resurrection is every day. The mighty power which God wrought in Christ when He raised Him from the dead can operate in our lives this moment…in the NOW… to deliver us from the problems of life that would hold us down (Romans 8:11).

Jesus said, "Unless I die I will be alone—a single seed. But my death will produce many new wheat kernels—a plentiful harvest of new lives" *(John 12:24 TLB)*. The resurrection of Jesus Christ was not an accident. Jesus seeded for that miracle! You don't get something for nothing. Miracles can come when you have put in the seed of faith *(Matthew 17:20)*. Every time you love, that's a seed of faith. Every time you give, that's a seed of faith. Every time you pray for someone, that's a seed of faith.

When you sow a seed of faith, you can sow a seed of resurrection from the problem you are facing. Jesus went to the cross for our victory in every moment of Christian living through His resurrection.

In PSALMS...
He Is the Lord, Our Shepherd

DAVID IS SOMETIMES called the shepherd king. He said, "The Lord is my shepherd; I shall not want" *(Psalm 23:1)*. Note the words "*my* shepherd." David based his relationship with God on a personal experience with the Lord. He communed with God as he led his father's sheep to pasture, and he would sing psalms and rejoice in the Lord.

Shepherds are close to their sheep. David knew his sheep and called each of them by name. They knew his voice and they responded to him. Jesus said, "I am the good shepherd, and know my sheep, and am known of mine" *(John 10:14)*. Salvation through the Lord, our Shepherd, is a personal experience...one where Christ knows you by name and you know Him. You walk hand-in-hand together and you speak with one another with familiarity and understanding. From your heart you can say, "The Lord is *MY* Shepherd, *MY* personal Savior, and Lord of *MY* life."

I shall not want! A good shepherd provides for *ALL* the needs of his flock. So many people think that you get saved only to go to heaven...*someday.* But the Lord knows that we *live* between now and heaven-going time!

"I used to think," confessed one man, "that God was interested only in my soul—that nebulous area of our human makeup that no one is able to describe, and yet everyone has. I wondered, doesn't Jesus have anything to say about what I eat or what I wear or the work I do?"

The ministry of Jesus, our Shepherd, is geared to meet the needs of the whole man in any area of his life. Philippians 4:19 says: "MY God shall supply *ALL* your need according to his riches in glory by Christ Jesus!"

When the man with a withered hand came to Jesus with a physical need, Jesus did not say, "I want to teach you something spiritual. I will give you grace to bear it." Jesus said, "Stretch forth thine hand," and *the man's hand was restored.*

Confronted with the hungry multitude, Jesus didn't attempt to teach them some spiritual law. He took the lad's lunch, blessed and multiplied it, and used it to *satisfy their hunger.*

Likewise, when Christ meets us in the area of our spirit, He does not leave us bound. He steps over to where we are and says, *Thy sins be forgiven*.

Jesus as the Lord, our Shepherd, is the Great Provider of all of life.

In PROVERBS and ECCLESIASTES... He Is Our Wisdom

SOLOMON WAS YOUNG and inexperienced when he came to the throne inherited from his father David. Yet he was expected to assume the full responsibilities of the great kingdom.

Solomon loved the Lord and was waiting before Him when the Lord appeared to Solomon in a dream and said, "Ask what I shall give thee." Solomon felt his total dependence upon God, saying, "I am but a little child: I know not how to go out or come in...give therefore thy servant an understanding heart to judge thy people, that I may discern between good and bad" *(1 Kings 3:5,7,9)*.

Solomon's request pleased God very much. He not only granted Solomon's unselfish request but also gave him "fringe benefits" of riches and honor for which he did not even ask! Solomon was a living example of the truth Jesus taught: "Seek ye first the kingdom of God, and his righteousness; and all these things shall be added unto you" *(Matthew 6:33).* There was none like unto Solomon in wisdom, riches, and splendor.

When Jesus preached to the multitude He said, "Behold, a greater than Solomon is here" *(Luke 11:31).* Those who would seek wisdom will go to Jesus Christ, "in whom are hid all the treasures of wisdom and knowledge" *(Colossians 2:3).*

The importance of wisdom in the believer's everyday life cannot be overestimated. For, like Solomon, we are run up against problems that we cannot solve within ourselves. But God was not partial to Solomon. The Bible says, "If any of you lack wisdom, let him ask of God...and it shall be given him" *(James 1:5).*

In the SONG OF SOLOMON...
He Is Our Lover and Bridegroom

OUTSTANDING IN THIS BOOK is the Bridegroom's love for His bride: "I am the rose of Sharon, and the lily of the valleys. As the lily among thorns, so is my love among the daughters" *(Song of Solomon 2:1–2)*. The Bridegroom is Jesus Christ and His bride is the Church.

Even in the Church's unperfected state, Christ loves her. In herself she is full of faults, but in Him she is "blameless and harmless" *(Philippians 2:15)*.

At this moment, the courtship between Christ and the Church is in progress. The Holy Spirit, who speaks not of himself but of Christ, is gathering out the faithful believers from among the nations of the world, getting ready for the marriage supper of the Lamb. The time soon is coming when Christ will call for His bride.

"I go to prepare a place for you," Jesus said, "and if I go and prepare a place for you, I will come again, and receive you unto myself; that where I am, there ye may be also" *(John 14:2–3)*.

Today we look with keen anticipation toward Christ's coming. The Word says in 1 John 3:3, "And every man that hath this hope in him purifieth himself, even as he is pure."

The most effective Christian is not the person who gets so "other-worldly" and loses himself in the raptures of the future that he forgets about the place where he lives NOW. Christ's second coming gives us not only our hope but also our present task. It is the greatest of incentives to purity. For knowing the glorious event that is in store for us, we do everything within our power to be ready for it and to help those about us to be prepared also. Oh, the joy of being ready to meet our Lover and Bridegroom, Jesus Christ!

In ISAIAH...
He Is the Prince of Peace

ISAIAH PROPHESIED, SAYING, "For unto us a child is born...his name shall be called Wonderful, Counsellor, the mighty God, the everlasting Father, the Prince of Peace" *(Isaiah 9:6).*

When Jesus was born in Bethlehem the angels sang, "On earth peace, good will toward men" *(Luke 2:14)*. In the person of God's Son, Jesus, we can see the whole man and what God wants us to be. He is the embodiment of peace and goodwill on earth. During Christ's ministry He brought peace—to troubled hearts, to a troubled world. And it is Christ's coming into our hearts today that can give us peace, for "being justified by faith, we have peace with God through our Lord Jesus Christ" *(Romans 5:1)*.

As Christ was preparing to leave His disciples to go back to His Heavenly Father, every word He spoke was weighted with significance. He said, "Peace I leave with you, my peace I give unto you: not as the world giveth, give I unto you. Let not your heart be troubled, neither let it be afraid" *(John 14:27)*. The Prince of Peace left an invaluable inheritance to all who believe on Him. Money cannot buy it, nor can it be taken from us. His peace provides contentment and calmness even in the midst of confusion and turmoil.

The Apostle Paul said, "Let the peace of God *rule* in your hearts," which implies that we must consciously allow His peace to rule. It is easy to be caught up in the turbulence of our times. Sometimes it takes a strong effort of the will to reject thoughts of anxiety and worry. But Isaiah 26:3 says, "Thou wilt keep him in perfect peace, whose mind is stayed on thee: because he trusteth in thee." Peace is an internal condition of the heart that results from an abiding relationship with the Prince of Peace.

In JEREMIAH and LAMENTATIONS... He Is Our Weeping Prophet

JEREMIAH WAS A PROPHET who carried his people on his heart. His generation had broken their vital relationship with God. Jeremiah was so concerned about their spiritual welfare that He wept, "Oh that my head were waters, and mine eyes a fountain of tears, that I might weep day and night for the slain of the daughter of my people" (*Jeremiah 9:1*).

I remember when I was a little boy in Sunday school, the teacher would say, "Oral, quote a verse of Scripture," and I would jump up and say, "Jesus wept." Then I'd laugh and sit down. At that time, I had no idea what I was saying.

But since I have been grown and become a serious Christian, I have come to realize that Jesus Christ is our Weeping Prophet. He wept. He wept with compassion for those who sorrowed over the death of Lazarus. He wept in pity over Jerusalem because of what was to come upon the people *(John 11:35; Luke 19.41)*.

Today there is a great need for those who will weep for lost humanity. If Zion does not travail, the Scripture teaches, sons and daughters will not be brought forth. The Psalmist said, "No man cared for my soul" *(Psalm 142:4)*. These heart-rending words were uttered thousands of years ago, but they are not out of date. Ministers and doctors hear firsthand accounts from people every day who are oppressed with the daily cares of life and whose hearts give forth the same cry, *No one cares!* They long for someone to be concerned about them and their problems.

John 7:37 says there is One who cares—Jesus, the Weeping Prophet—who said, "If any man thirst, let him come unto me, and drink." When no one else in the world seems to care about you, you can look to Jesus. He cares. His hands are outstretched in invitation to come and to cast your cares and burdens upon Him *(1 Peter 5:7)*.

In EZEKIEL...
He Is the Wonderful
Four-Faced Man

"AS FOR THE LIKENESS of their faces, they four had the face of a man" *(Ezekiel 1:10)*.

Ezekiel saw a vision of the Four-faced Man when he was in captivity in Babylon—a vision of Jesus Christ and His precious redemptive work for all mankind. This vision inspired Ezekiel with the responsibility of the hour, to keep before the people their sins and to sustain the faith of the exiles.

God came to other great men in the Bible and gave them like visions when they were faced with difficult tasks. A vision of Christ and His holiness can stir our hearts and make us draw closer to Him. How can man see a vision of Jesus without being moved to action?

Moses saw "him who is invisible," and it caused him to turn his back upon the pleasures of Egypt and cast his lot with the people of God to be their deliverer *(Hebrews 11:27).*

When Isaiah, who was faced with the task of leading the people back to God, saw the heavenly vision, he cried, "Woe is me! for I am undone... mine eyes have seen the King, the Lord of hosts." When the Lord said, "Whom shall I send, and who will go for us?" Isaiah answered, "Here am I; send me" *(Isaiah 6:5,8).*

What a tremendous advantage we can have when we are able to see spiritually. The Bible says, "The natural man receiveth not the things of the Spirit of God: for they are foolishness unto him: neither can he know them, because they are spiritually discerned" *(1 Corinthians 2:14).* When we are hemmed in by trouble on every side, if we are able to see with the eyes of our inner self, we can see God...people...life...and even our problems. But above all, we can see the right answers!

In DANIEL...
He Is the Fourth Man in the Fiery Furnace

SEVERAL HUNDRED YEARS before Jesus Christ was born, Jerusalem was destroyed by the armies of the mighty King Nebuchadnezzar from Babylon. Young Hebrew men like Shadrach, Meshach, and Abednego were taken hundreds of miles across the deserts to the city of Babylon, captives of a heathen king.

Ushered inside the great city, the three youths heard the sound of music and learned that they were required to fall down and worship a huge burnished gold image of King Nebuchadnezzar. But they refused, saying they knelt before the Lord God only. Enraged, the king ordered them to be thrown into the fiery furnace, saying, "Who is that God that shall deliver you out of my hands?" *(Daniel 3:15)*

These young men came face-to-face with the inescapable fact of life that true faith will be tried. Everyone who follows Christ may face some type of ultimatum—either bow or burn. Bow down and compromise what the Bible teaches, or you may have no influence. But what does man gain by compromising? It does not have the power to satisfy him. On the other hand, what he gets by faith he can keep.

The Hebrews' answer was confident and full of faith: "If it be so, our God whom we serve is able to deliver us from the burning fiery furnace" *(Daniel 3:17)*. These young men were not whistling in the dark, trying to bolster their courage. They were speaking out of knowledge and experience. The record of their God was that He is able.

The three men were bound and cast into the furnace that had been heated seven times hotter than usual. The king stood by, and after a while he looked in. When he did, his hair seemingly stood on end. He cried to his counselors, "Did not we cast three men bound into the midst of the fire?"

They answered, "True, O King."

He said, "Lo, I see four men loose, walking in the midst of the fire, and they have no hurt; and the form of the fourth is like the Son of God" *(Daniel 3:24–25)*.

The Fourth Man, Jesus Christ, delivered the three men without a hair of their heads being singed or even the smell of fire being upon them. He went through the furnace with them!

Perhaps you and I will never stand in front of a furnace burning with literal fire, but in our sphere we will have our fiery furnace experiences. In these times, we can find that the Fourth Man is with us. Through every temptation, every trial of life, we can say with the same confidence the three Hebrews had: "If it be so, our God whom we serve is able to deliver us from the burning fiery furnace!"

In HOSEA...
He Is the Eternal Husband Forever Married to the Backslider

IN THE BIBLE, the closest of all human relationships is that which exists between husband and wife. The Lord chose this beautiful comparison to depict the relationship of love and devotion that exists between Him and His people.

Hosea's heartbreak over the harlotry of his wife is symbolic of God's anguish and heartache over Israel's unfaithfulness in departing from Him. Between sobs, Hosea magnifies God's love and tries to help them understand the true nature of God. The prophet keeps repeating the Lord's call to return. Even in the face of their persistent backslidings, God in love says, "How shall I give thee up…mine heart is turned within me, my repentings [compassions] are kindled together. I will heal their backsliding, I will love them freely," He offers, "if they will return" *(Hosea 11:8; 14:4)*. What a vivid picture of the steadfast love of God!

Hosea was certainly one of the most Christ-like of all the prophets of the Old Testament. He reminds us of Christ who "came unto his own, and his own received him not" *(John 1:11)*. Hosea shows us that sin is not just putting some other god in God's place, but sin is like adultery. It is forsaking the One who loves you with an everlasting love. Hosea wept, "I will betroth thee unto me for ever" *(Hosea 2:19)*. In him we see Christ as the Eternal Husband Forever Married to the Backslider.

In JOEL...
He Is the Baptizer in the Holy Spirit

"AND IT SHALL COME to pass afterward, that I will pour out my spirit upon all flesh" *(Joel 2:28).* "Afterward" here means *in the last days.*

The signs of the last days are evident all around us, but I think what impresses me most is the work of the Spirit in the world today. The Holy Spirit in the NOW is beginning a new march across the earth. In the midst of the wickedness of these last days, God's power is coming against the devil's power. To match the destructive power of Satan, Christ's Church is being equipped with an understanding and workable knowledge of the Holy Spirit and the nine supernatural gifts of the Spirit *(1 Corinthians 12:1–11).* We are learning better how to apply the power of the Holy Spirit to practical problems that we face in our daily existence.

Christ is the Baptizer in the Holy Spirit. John baptized those who came to him "with water unto repentance." But he said, "He that cometh after me is mightier than I, whose shoes I am not worthy to bear: he shall baptize you with the Holy [Spirit], and with fire" *(Matthew 3:31)*.

Christ is pouring out the baptism in the Holy Spirit in all churches. He is not looking at the name over the church door or at the church affiliation of individuals before giving them this marvelous gift. He is looking at hungry hearts. Christ's answer for people's needs today is the same as it was for His discouraged and defeated disciples when He was about to leave them and return to His throne in glory: "Behold, I send the promise of my Father upon you: but tarry ye...until ye be endued with power from on high" *(Luke 24:49)*.

The baptism in the Holy Spirit can cause Jesus, who is love, to EXPLODE in our hearts with power from on high so that we are living witnesses of His love.

In AMOS...
He Is Our Burden-Bearer

"WOE TO THEM that are at ease in. Zion, and trust in the mountain of Samaria," cried the Prophet Amos *(Amos 6:1)*. No one seemed to care about God or His work. Even the priest did not want Amos to prophesy God's warning to the people of the destruction and heartache that would come to them because of their sins. But Amos, a young shepherd, had his commission straight from God and he would not keep quiet. Amos' great concern for his people's spiritual condition was a real burden on his heart. He became their burden-bearer and prayed for God to spare them.

Jesus Christ is described as our Burden-bearer. Isaiah 53:4 says, "Surely he hath borne our griefs, and carried our sorrows." The sins and heartaches of the whole world were upon Him when He went to the cross and paid humanity's sin-debt. He proved how very much He loves us.

Jesus walked every foot of life as a man, facing the same type of human needs and frustrations that we do. It was in this arena of struggle that He said, "Come unto me, all ye that labour and are heavy laden, and I will give you rest… Learn of me…for my yoke is easy, and my burden is light" *(Matthew 11:28–30)*.

The good news of Christ's Gospel is that we don't have to struggle under the load of life's burdens, trying to handle them by ourselves.

Jesus had probably made yokes for oxen in His father's carpenter shop many times. In this Scripture, it seems He may have been referring to the Eastern way of breaking young oxen to the yoke. They often place a young ox in the yoke next to a stronger, more mature ox. The yoke is placed closest to the stronger ox. This way, the young ox carries the load, but the strain is not as heavy because the stronger, older ox pulls the heavy end of the load. Christ's yoke is easy and His burden is light because HE carries the heavy end!

In OBADIAH...
He Is Our Savior

OBADIAH PROPHESIED A Savior who would come to deliver the people. "But upon mount Zion shall be deliverance," he said, and "saviours shall come up on mount Zion to judge the mount of Esau; and the kingdom shall be the Lord's" *(Obadiah 17 and 21).*

It was said of Christ: "Thou shalt call his name JESUS: for he shall save his people from their sins" *(Matthew 1:21).*

The name JESUS literally means THE SAVIOR. A more fitting name could not have been given Him. For John 3:17 says, "God sent not his son into the world to condemn the world; but that the world through him might be saved."

Again it is written, "There is none other name under heaven given among men, whereby we must be saved" *(Acts 4:12).*

Christianity means salvation—wholeness—for every area of your life—soul, mind, and body. Scripture tells us that Jesus came to regenerate us, transform us, and make us a new creation, as only He can do.

Jesus Christ did not come to shorten our lives. He came to save them. He wants us to live out our days on this earth so that we can be witnesses for Him. He wants us to have strong souls, strong minds, and strong bodies. He wants to prosper us financially, to multiply the seed we sow, to gladden our hearts, to lift up our spirits, and to give us strength for the responsibilities that He has entrusted to our care.

God sent His Son to restore all that the devil had taken from us, to take out of us what the devil had put in, and to put back what he had stolen. Through Jesus we are recreated—a "new creature" *(2 Corinthians 5:17)*. What a Savior!

In JONAH...
He Is the Great Foreign Missionary

JONAH MAY BE the first book on foreign missions ever written. God told Jonah, "Arise, go to Nineveh, the great city, and cry against it; for their wickedness is come up before me" *(Jonah 1:2)*.

Jonah ran from the presence of God. He didn't want to go to Nineveh. These people were not Jewish people. As far as Jonah was concerned, they were heathen people. But that is why God wanted him to go there. They needed the Lord. They would turn to God if someone would go tell them about Him.

In trying to escape from God's call, Jonah had an experience in the bottom of the fish's belly that made him willing to go to these people. Jesus likened Jonah's experience to the three days He spent in the heart of the earth *(Matthew 12:40).* Without Christ's resurrection, all would have been in vain. If Jonah had stayed in the fish's belly, all would have been lost as far as Nineveh was concerned. But God brought him out, and Jonah was willing to share his God with others outside his nation.

According to the Bible, we are ALL witnesses of our Lord. Every one of us! When you read the New Testament and consider the witness of men like Philip and Stephen, you can find that there is not much difference between the witness of one who is a preacher and one who is a layman *(Acts 6:8; 8:5–8).*

Jesus Himself said this would be true: "Ye shall receive power, after that the Holy [Spirit] is come upon you," He said, "and ye shall be witnesses unto me" *(Acts 1:8).*

Naturally, there are functions of the ministry that are set apart for preachers. But essentially the gospel of Christ is on a personal level…one-on-one. It's Jesus and the individual. It is someone loving

God and applying that love to others. Through the power of the Spirit, every believer can give to his generation the light and life of Jesus.

In MICAH…
He Is the Messenger
with Beautiful Feet

MICAH WAS THE BEARER of the good news of the coming millennial reign of Jesus Christ on the earth when all will be peace: "They shall beat their swords into plowshares, and their spears into pruninghooks: nation shall not lift up a sword against nation, neither shall they learn war any more" *(Micah 4:3)*.

He also had the good news of the advent of Jesus Christ, the One who would pardon iniquity. "Who is a God like unto thee, that pardoneth iniquity, and passeth by the transgression of the remnant of his heritage? he retaineth not his anger for ever, because he delighteth in mercy" *(Micah 7:18)*.

Micah was a messenger with beautiful feet, for the Bible tells us, "How beautiful upon the mountains are the feet of him that bringeth good tidings, that publisheth peace...that publisheth salvation; that saith unto Zion, Thy God reigneth" *(Isaiah 52:7)*.

When Christ was born, the greatest news of all time came fresh from heaven's news presses and was broadcast to the world by an angel courier. The angel's words thrilled with excitement: "Fear not: for, behold, I bring you good tidings of great joy, which shall be to all people. For unto you is born...a Saviour, which is Christ the Lord" *(Luke 2:10–11)*.

When Jesus came, He found a world of impossibilities. Humanity was bound by naturalism. The power of God was conspicuously absent from the ways of men. Therefore, men were not able to solve their problems. They came up against failure with no recourse. Their sick often lay by the highwayside.

Christ was indeed the Messenger with Beautiful Feet, for He marched into the arena of human suffering, proclaiming the message of God's love. He brought thrilling news of deliverance:

"The Spirit of the Lord is upon me," He said, "because he hath anointed me to preach the gospel to the poor; he hath sent me to heal the brokenhearted, to preach deliverance to the captives, and recovering of sight to the blind, to set at liberty them that are bruised" *(Luke 4 18)*.

The message that Christ brings is to soothe the troubled brow, calm the angry mind, and bring healing and wholeness to man.

In NAHUM...
He Is Our Avenger

NAHUM WAS A PROPHET of comfort to Israel. To his oppressed people who were under the enemy's yoke, Nahum's first words were those of comfort and hope: "God is jealous, and the Lord revengeth... The Lord will take vengeance on his adversaries, and he reserveth wrath for his enemies. The Lord is good, a strong hold in the day of trouble; and he knoweth them that trust in him" *(Nahum 1:2,7)*.

Christianity gives a new dimension to a person's life. When Jesus' enemies came to arrest Him in the Garden of Gethsemane, Simon Peter unsheathed his sword and whacked off the ear of the high priest's servant. But Jesus quickly restored the man's ear and rebuked Peter, saying, "Put up thy sword...for all they that take the sword shall perish with the sword" *(Matthew 26:52)*.

Christ demonstrated that Christianity is not a religion of the sword but of healing and deliverance. He is our Avenger. Our hands are to be opened to bless others. Christ taught us that God is with us and fights our battles: "Dearly beloved, avenge not yourselves, but rather give place unto wrath... Vengeance is mine: I will repay, saith the Lord" *(Romans 12:19)*.

In HABAKKUK...
He Is the Evangelist
Pleading for a Revival

HABAKKUK'S BURDEN and prayer was for a revival. "O Lord...revive thy work in the midst of the years," he prayed, "in the midst of the years make known; in wrath remember mercy" *(Habakkuk 3:2)*.

Jesus Christ lit the torch of evangelism. The Father sent Jesus; Jesus sends us. He is the Evangelist Pleading for a Revival: "Say not ye, There are yet four months, and then cometh harvest? behold, I say unto you, Lift up your eyes, and look on the fields; for they are white already to harvest" *(John 4:35).*

A tourist stood in the beautiful Olympic Stadium in Athens, Greece. His guide explained how the Olympian games start in that stadium. "A torch is lighted in Olympia," he said. "A runner takes that torch and runs all the way to this stadium. Here the fire from that torch is applied to another one, and another runner takes it and starts with it to the ship that is to carry the Greek team overseas where the games are to be played. That fire is never allowed to go out until the games are over and the winners announced!"

Likewise, Christ applied the torch of His own personality and conquering Spirit to the lives of His disciples. Soon, these 12 became 120. Before long, the 120 torches became 3,000. The 3,000 became 5,000. And the multiplication kept on until His enemies exclaimed, "All Jerusalem is filled with this doctrine" *(Acts 5:28).*

Christ said, "Ye are the light of the world" *(Matthew 5:14).* We are His torchbearers, and that flame must never go out until "the game is over and the winners announced."

In ZEPHANIAH...
He Is the Lord Mighty to Save

ZEPHANIAH POINTS US to the Lord who is mighty to save. "The Lord thy God in the midst of thee is mighty; he will save, he will rejoice over thee with joy; he will rest in his love, he will joy over thee with singing" *(Zephaniah 3:17)*.

Christ is a mighty Savior from sin and from its dominion over us. The Apostle Paul wrote concerning Christ, "He is able also to save them to the uttermost that come unto God by him" *(Hebrews 7:25)*.

Paul wrote from his own personal experience with Christ. Not only did Jesus Christ forgive Paul's sins, but also He broke the power of sin over him. Jesus changed the pattern of this man's life so that he who had been walking in darkness, in hate, and in vengeance now began to walk in the light, in love, and in consideration of his fellow men. All the hate he had in his heart was gone, and God replaced it with love.

This marvelous work of grace can be part of the life of every believer. The Bible does not bear out the theory that it is "normal" to live a defeated

Christian life. Jesus Christ promises us complete victory over sin. The Bible says that when He forgives us our sins, He delivers us from sin's control. Through Christ's power we can overcome daily, to live a new life, to go in a new direction, because "greater is [the Christ who] is in you, than [the devil who] is in the world" *(1 John 4:4).*

Christ's power can enable us to change from a person filled with defeat and frustration to a happy, harmonious person at peace with God. He is the Lord Mighty to Save!

In HAGGAI...
He Is the Restorer of the Lost Heritage

HAGGAI ENCOURAGED HIS people who had come back from captivity to work and restore the temple of God which had been lost, and there to worship the Lord of hosts. True worship of God was their heritage.

The foundation of the temple had been laid 15 years previously, but there it stopped. They had returned from captivity, but not to the building of God's House. The people were in a state of lethargy, and Haggai sought to strengthen their hearts. He cried, "Be strong, all ye people of the land, saith the Lord, and work: for I am with you, saith the Lord of hosts" *(Haggai 2:4)*. Haggai's message was effective. The people obeyed his voice, and the building of the temple was resumed. Their heritage was restored.

In the beginning all of God's creations were, in His words, "very good." When God created man, He not only placed him in a perfect environment but also gave him many magnificent gifts, such as the gift of His own spiritual and moral likeness, the gift of understanding and communication with God, and the gift of the power of dominion *(Genesis 1:27–28)*.

The first negative act in creation was by the devil: to get man to reject God and the way He had made him—a spiritual being. But God's act to counteract the devil was absolutely positive. He gave man His greatest Gift of all—His Son, Jesus Christ! "He led captivity captive, and GAVE GIFTS unto men" *(Ephesians 4:8)*. Christ was God's greatest gift to man because He came to earth to recapture the gifts of God that man had lost…to regain all the first Adam had lost that He might give it to every man.

How did Jesus do this? He began in the Spirit, for the Spirit conceived man in the beginning, and the Holy Spirit conceived Jesus *(Matthew 1:20)*. This is why Jesus said, "Ye must be born again. Except a man be born...of the Spirit, he cannot enter into the kingdom of God" *(John 3:7,5)*.

Jesus didn't say, "Ye must be born of the mind... or of the body." *Ye must be born of the spirit!* He recaptured the new birth so that man could be reborn in the spiritual and moral likeness of God. The experience of conversion can be a reintegration of the *withness* and *nowness* of God in a person's entire personality—a restoration of all the gifts of God which were lost!

In ZECHARIAH...
He Is the Fountain Opened to the House of David for Sin and Uncleanness

"IN THAT DAY," said the prophet Zechariah, "there shall be a fountain opened to the house of David and to the inhabitants of Jerusalem for sin and for uncleanness" *(Zechariah 13:1)*.

Jesus told the little woman of Samaria at Jacob's well, "Whosoever drinketh of this water shall thirst again: but whosoever drinketh of the water that I shall give him shall never thirst; but the water that I shall give him shall be in him a well of water springing up into everlasting life" *(John 4:13–14)*.

At first, the woman thought Christ was talking about literal water. But when she understood that He was speaking of the Fountain Opened to the House of David for sin and for uncleanness, her soul was thrilled to its depths. She drank of the Living Water and ran into the city to tell others that they might come and drink also.

You can understand why the woman left her water pot behind. She didn't need it any longer! She now had a whole well of the water of eternal life springing up in her heart. All those days of searching and reaching out for love and trying to fill the thirst of her life were now over because she had quenched her thirst in God's love.

This fountain is still springing up with everlasting life. Christ's invitation constantly goes forth,

"If any man thirst, let him come unto me, and drink" *(John 7:37)*.

In MALACHI...
He Is the Sun of Righteousness Rising with Healing in His Wings

MALACHI POINTED THE people to the coming healing Christ: "Unto you that fear my name shall the Sun of righteousness arise with healing in his wings" *(Malachi 4:2)*.

Matthew 8:16–17 relates this story concerning Christ's healing work: "When the even was come, they brought unto him many that were possessed with devils: and he cast out the spirits with his word, and healed all that were sick: That it might be fulfilled which was spoken by Esaias the prophet, saying, Himself took our infirmities, and bare our sicknesses."

The man Jesus Christ, this incarnate Son of God, came to make men in His likeness—*whole*.

When I first started praying for the sick, I thought healing was primarily for the body, for physical illnesses. Gradually the Lord showed me in the Bible that healing is for the whole man. It's for the body, the soul, and the mind. It's also for the problems we face.

Sickness takes many forms. We usually think of sickness being in the form of cancer, pneumonia, or something like that. But anything that brings disharmony, discomfort, or distress—either physically, mentally, or spiritually—is a form of illness. Sin, fear, loneliness, and other issues can be a form of sickness, because the whole person—the total personality—can be affected by anything that happens to any of its parts.

From that standpoint, we can see that people need the healing touch of Jesus Christ, the Sun of Righteousness rising with healing in His wings.

In MATTHEW...
He Is the Messiah

EVER SINCE GOD made the first promise of a Redeemer, the human race looked for Christ— the Messiah, *the Anointed One.* At last the time came. Matthew records the genealogy and the birth of the long-promised Messiah:

"Behold, a virgin shall be with child, and shall bring forth a son, and they shall call his name Emmanuel, which being interpreted is, God with us" *(Matthew 1:23)*.

God with us! What a contrast to the watered-down version of Christianity where God is an unmoved mover of the universe, a divine intelligence behind it all.

So, God sent a living personal being. Jesus Christ, the Messiah, came to the earth for one purpose—to help people, to meet their needs: "God *anointed* Jesus of Nazareth with the Holy [Spirit] and with power: who went about doing good, and healing all that were oppressed of the devil; for God was with him" *(Acts 10:38)*.

In order for God to live as a person in this world through His Son Jesus Christ, He had to experience suffering. For "man that is born of a woman is of few days, and full of trouble" *(Job 14:1)*. Therefore, Jesus Christ knows every dark lane in life. Every bright moment. Every low valley. Every high experience. Our Lord has been all along the way. He's been tested like we are tested. He's been tempted like we are tempted.

He's been down the road. He knows what it is. He knows what it means to be a human being, to feel like a human being, to live in a real world.

You can take John 3:16–17 and summarize the gospel story in the three verbs—God *loved*… God *gave*…that people might be *saved*. Every one of these verbs is costly. Each is a word of action, of involvement at the deepest level. God is not only *FOR* us. Emmanuel means God is also in this world *WITH* us. The Messiah conquered the world so that we might conquer NOW through HIM!

In MARK…
He Is the Wonder-Worker

MARK CONCENTRATED HIS Gospel on the works of Jesus Christ rather than on His words. Everywhere Jesus is seen as the Wonder-worker.

In that day the Romans worshipped power. They loved parades and displays of military might. Mark was saying to them, "You love power. You like great wonders. Then I will present to you the Wonder-worker, Jesus Christ."

Isaiah prophesied that Jesus Christ would be called Wonderful—a wonder.

Mark recorded miracle after miracle that Jesus performed. He broke up funeral processions, robbed the grave of its victim, walked across the storm-tossed Sea of Galilee, healed the sick, opened blinded eyes, unstopped deaf ears, made the dumb to speak, and the crippled to walk.

Jesus never called the things He did miracles. The writers of the Gospels call them miracles, but Jesus called them "the *works* of my Father" *(John 10:37)*. And He said, "Greater works than these shall [you] do" *(John 14:12)*.

The meaning of that is rich and precious today. When we have needs that are insurmountable, problems that are baffling, we have access to God and His wonderful works. He can come to us here in the NOW.

Jesus was telling us that miracles are not a sometime thing or a onetime thing or some sort of magic. They're the *continuous* action of the Father's love, concern, and power for people. God meant His works to continue. The works of our Father can be a part of our hope, our expectation, and our existence.

Miracles are possible in the NOW because they are simply the works of the Father continuing in our lives!

In LUKE...
He Is the Son of Man

THE BIRTH OF JESUS CHRIST was supernatural *(Matthew 1:20)*. He was born of a virgin. This is what we call "the virgin birth." He received His body and human features from His mother Mary. But the divine part of Jesus was conceived by the Holy Spirit, so that He became the Son of man from Mary and Son of God from the Holy Spirit.

This is a great mystery for the intellect to comprehend. It has to be accepted and believed by faith *(1 Corinthians 2:14)*. On the one hand, Jesus was total man...so much man it was as if He were not God. On the other hand, He was total God...so much God it was as if He were not man. Jesus was Son of man and Son of God.

The key phrase of Luke's Gospel is "Son of man." His picture of our Lord emphasizes Christ's humanity—His love and compassion for the poor, the suffering, the sinful. Luke writes, "The Son of man is come to seek and to save that which was lost" *(Luke 19:10).*

It is easy to make Jesus so divine that we forget He was also human…one of us!

"Wherefore in all things it behoved him [Jesus] to be made like unto his brethren, that he might be a merciful and faithful high priest… For in that he himself hath suffered being tempted, he is able to succour them that are tempted" *(Hebrews 2:17–18).*

Jesus was man when He was born a baby in Bethlehem and cradled in His mother's arms. But He was God when He spoke words of authority to the doctors and lawyers in the temple.

He was man as He lay sleeping in the boat that stormy night on Galilee. But He was God when He stood and said, "Peace, be still."

Jesus was man when He shed bitter, salty tears at the graveside of his friend Lazarus. But He was God when He said, "Lazarus, come forth!"

He was man when they nailed His body to the cross. But He was God when He said, "It is finished."

Jesus was man when they took His bleeding body and put it in a tomb. But He was God when He arose from the dead.

Jesus in His humanity is God coming to people where we are...as we are...in the form of our need!

In JOHN...
He Is the Son of God

JOHN BEAUTIFULLY PORTRAYS the divinity and humanity of Jesus Christ. "The Word was made flesh," he writes, "and dwelt among us (and we beheld his glory)" *(John 1:14)*.

God is found in the reality of living—not in abstract philosophy. Christ's message first was declared to people who had no time-saving devices, no knowledge of sanitation, few pleasures, and little freedom. They were people who labored hard, who came home tired and still had to meet the needs of their families. Yet, in the midst of this scene, Christ—the Son of God—commanded peace, health, joy, and life.

Christ came to us who live on *earth*. His perfection is for those who grow irritable. His

Golden Rule is for us who have prying neighbors or unkind associates. His peace is for us who struggle with tensions. His courage is for us who are timid and afraid.

His deity cannot be disputed. Even His enemies said, "Never man spake like this man" *(John 7:46).* When He was nailed to the cross, the centurion who had been in charge of the operation cried, "Truly this was the Son of God" *(Matthew 27:54).*

After thrilling hearts with one incident after another that pointed out the deity of Christ, John concludes by saying, "Many other signs truly did Jesus in the presence of his disciples which are not written in this book: but these are written, that ye might believe that Jesus is the Christ, the Son of God; and that believing ye might have life through his name" *(John 20:30–31).*

In ACTS...
He Is the Holy Spirit Moving and Working Among Men

LUKE IS THE writer of the Acts of the Apostles. He continues the account of Christianity begun in the Gospel which bears his name. In Luke, he tells what Jesus *"began* both to do and teach;" in the Acts, what Jesus *continued* to do and teach through His Holy Spirit which He promised to send *(Acts 1:8)*.

Some people look upon the book of Acts as just a historical record of the happenings of the Early Church. But it's more than that... Oh, so much more! For it is around the book of Acts that we can orient ourselves toward the Lord Jesus Christ.

The four Gospels—Matthew, Mark, Luke, and John—are about the earthly life of our Lord. But the book of Acts tells us of the reproduction of the life of Jesus in His followers—people who had weaknesses and made mistakes, but who came to believe on Christ and who went on to be like Him. The Christ who was reproduced in them can be the SAME CHRIST who is reproduced in us.

The book of Acts breathes with the power of the risen Christ. The world thought it had killed Jesus, but it soon discovered that He had risen in a hundred different places. It found that He reappeared through His disciples' lives. Instead of destroying Him, it had multiplied Him many times over. After His resurrection, Jesus transmitted His nature and power to His disciples. We see this power flowing through the early Christians *(John 7:38–39)*. They preached with resurrection power. The people let their faith go to God and marvelous miracles were wrought.

The book of Acts has a beginning but no logical ending...because it hasn't ended. This book is still being written in the acts of the people of God in THIS generation and will be until the Lord returns. For through the Holy Spirit, it is the same as—and even greater than—having Jesus with us in the flesh. For we can have Jesus' personal presence and power moving and working through us at all times.

In ROMANS...
He Is the Justifier

THE GREAT DOCTRINE of Paul's Epistle to the Romans is justification by faith. Though "all have sinned and come short of the glory of God," Paul writes, we are "justified freely by his grace through the redemption that is in Christ Jesus" *(Romans 3:23–24)*.

Nearly 600 years before the birth of Christ, the Prophet Habakkuk introduced this tremendous truth—"The just shall live by his faith" *(Habakkuk 2:4; Romans 1:17)*. To appreciate the prophet's insight, we should remember that he was talking to people whose worship was almost wholly concerned with, and dependent upon, externals.

Habakkuk was perplexed because the religion of the people was not practical to the things in everyday human experience. It was then that faith was revealed to him as the working instrument of religion—the faith by which we can live, cope with our problems, and get our needs met.

Jesus constantly likened faith with a seed being planted to get a result. He said, "If ye have faith as a grain of mustard seed, ye shall say unto this mountain, Remove hence to yonder place; and it shall remove; and nothing shall be impossible unto you" *(Matthew 17:20)*.

This suggests that if you have faith as a seed, or if your believing becomes *seed-faith,* no matter how small it seems to be, it can meet needs and problems that appear as impossible as mountains before you. This is because each act of faith can be a seed planted and can be multiplied back to you many times in the form of your need.

Dependence upon any human instrument for the maintenance of our Christian life can fail. But the Bible says we are to live by faith…dependent upon GOD who is our Source. Faith in Him can sustain us. We can never do anything to be worthy of God's grace and blessings, nor can we attain to any righteousness by our own efforts *(Philippians 3:9).* The Christian life is the out-living of the in-living Christ—the Justifier.

In 1 & 2 CORINTHIANS…
He Is the Sanctifier

PAUL ESTABLISHED THE Church at Corinth. He had come into godless, corrupt Corinth—a place where there were thousands of temples filled with gods of all descriptions, where part of their worship was legalized religious prostitution—and he preached Jesus to them. They believed. Then Paul built this great church.

They got off to a magnificent start. Then corruption began to creep in. Paul's earnest exhortations were to prevent their relapse into the old life of sin. "Having therefore these promises, dearly beloved," he wrote, "let us cleanse ourselves from all filthiness of the flesh and spirit, perfecting holiness in the fear of God" *(2 Corinthians 7:1)*.

Hebrews 12:14 says, "Follow peace with all men, and holiness, without which no man shall see the Lord." All down through time, God commanded His people to be holy, for He is a holy God.

The Bible pulls no punches in discussing worldliness: "Love not the world, neither the things that are in the world. If any man love the world, the love of the Father is not in him. For all that is in the world, the lust of the flesh, and the lust of the eyes, and the pride of life, is not of the Father, but is of the world" *(1 John 2:15–16)*.

Worldliness is a love of sensual indulgences, pride, self-sufficiency, hatred. It is living as one pleases.

None of us can be holy in ourselves. That is why Paul wrote to "them that are sanctified in *Christ Jesus*"—to those who had consecrated themselves unto the Lord. "Ye are sanctified... ye are justified," Paul wrote, "in the name of the Lord Jesus" *(1 Corinthians 1:2; 6:11).*

Holiness is the fruit of a life-transforming experience of salvation...a commitment of our total lives to the Lord. It is a growing experience...a daily liberation of our inner man from impurities and selfish desires...a redirecting of our life into channels of unselfish service to God and man, born of love. Holiness is to be the natural by-product of a vital love relationship between us and Jesus Christ the Sanctifier.

In GALATIANS...
He Is the Redeemer from
the Curse of the Law

"CHRIST HATH REDEEMED us from the curse of the law, being made a curse for us: for it is written, Cursed is every one that hangeth on a tree" *(Galatians 3:13).*

Jesus Christ bore our sins in His body on the tree (cross). There He tasted death for every man, dying that we might live and be redeemed from the curse and the burden of sin. He opened up "a new and living way" *(Hebrews 10:20)*.

The Apostle Paul wrote:

"The law of the Spirit of life in Christ Jesus hath made me free from the law of sin and death. For what the law could not do, in that it was weak through the flesh, God sending his own Son in the likeness of sinful flesh, and for sin, condemned sin in the flesh: that the righteousness of the law might be fulfilled in us, who walk not after the flesh, but after the Spirit" *(Romans 8:2–4)*.

Christ said He did not come to do away with the Law but to fulfill it *(Matthew 5:17)*. He showed us a vast difference in Old Testament and New Testament living. For instance, in the Old Testament you received first, then you gave. To teach His ownership, God did things for people, and after they received, they were to give back to Him. It was a debt. They owed it. They owed God their time—the Sabbath; they owed Him their money—the tithe. Everything was something they owed to God. But the debt was too big; man could not pay it. When Jesus went to the cross, He paid that debt and redeemed us from the curse of the Law. He opened up a whole new dimension of love and giving.

Jesus changed the Old Testament custom of receiving and then giving...to giving first that you might receive *(Luke 6:38)*. Jesus teaches you to give, not as a debt you owe but as a seed you sow. Your giving is a seed you sow first, then you receive from God a miracle-harvest to meet your need.

This is a whole new framework of living. We can no longer give to God to pay a debt because Christ has already paid it. So we come out of the Old Testament with its heavy requirements into the joy of New Testament living. It makes Christianity understandable and a joy!

In EPHESIANS...
He Is the Christ of
Unsearchable Riches

WITH HUMILITY, PAUL, who refers to himself as "less than the least of all saints," tells how God chose him to preach the "unsearchable riches of Christ; and to make all men see what is the fellowship of the mystery, which from the beginning of the world hath been hid in God" *(Ephesians 3:7–9).*

There are many riches that are unsearchable because they are inaccessible, such as the pearls of the sea caves and the minerals of the ocean. Some are unsearchable because they are secret, such as a hidden treasure. No doubt, there are riches and depths in Christ which are yet above and beyond our grasp spiritually. But it is not in this sense that the riches of Christ are called unsearchable.

The doors of Christ's treasure-house are flung open wide so that all may enter. There is no veil of mystery to prevent a little child from seeing the beauty within. Christ's riches are unsearchable simply because they are so abundant and so varied that we can never measure or fully distinguish them.

Though millions have come to the cross of Christ, His saving grace does not diminish. His strength never fails. His grace is sufficient. His supply is inexhaustible. God's Word shows us that Christ is the way to life, to peace, to health and happiness—to all the human heart could ever desire!

In PHILIPPIANS...
He Is the God Who
Supplieth All Our Need

"MY GOD SHALL SUPPLY all your need according to his riches in glory by Christ Jesus" *(Philippians 4:19)*.

"My God..." It's awfully easy to look to people, rather than to God, and expect them to solve your problems. But it's hard when they let you down. It's so easy to get encouraged when there's prosperity in the land and things are good for you. And it's easy, too, to get discouraged when there's depression or recession in the land. But it can be a mistake to look at life this way because our Source is not other people and it's not the economy. The Bible says our Source is GOD!

"...shall supply." Jesus looks on our needs in a positive way. To Him, a need exists to be

met. "God *shall* supply." *Shall* is a strong word. Emphatic! In other words, the moment a need faces you, God's "shall-supply" promise can go into effect.

"...ALL your need." God's provision is total. Your needs, no matter what they are, are a legitimate claim you can have upon God's limitless resources for the need to be met in full! You can give God your best, as He says in Luke 6:38, then you can ask God for His best. This is scriptural.

"...according to his riches in glory." What a comparison! All our needs compared to God's inestimable riches in heaven! God controls all His sources of supply, both the expected and the unexpected.

You can get hung up at this point if you are not careful. Your need can appear to exceed God's abundance. But God is the same God in good times or bad times.

In Habakkuk 3:17–19, God is saying that though all the crops are destroyed and all the jobs fail, and all things that have to do with our material existence are taken away, we can still rejoice and be happy in the Lord. If we are looking to God who is our strength and our Source, we can go through it all without fear of things to come, without losing our faith, and without being denied the things that we have to have. God wants to take care of us!

"...by Christ Jesus." That means here in the NOW, there can be a source of power for our human needs, human problems, and human limitations. Why wring your hands when you face problems and necessities, when you can KNOW that God supplies...according to the power of the unlimited Christ!

In COLOSSIANS...
He Is the Fullness of the
Godhead Bodily

"AND HE IS before all things, and by him all things consist... For it pleased the Father that in him should all fulness dwell" *(Colossians 1:17,19)*.

God comes to us *as the Father.* He comes with the love and the protection, the security and the power of a father to supply our needs. Jesus taught us to pray by addressing God as, "Our Father which art in heaven" *(Matthew 6:9)*. The word "Father" referring to God was used this way by our Lord Jesus Christ to signify the closeness that He and God the Father had together.

God comes to us *through His Son, Jesus Christ.*

It is difficult for us to visualize God as a spirit because our minds are conditioned to sight, sound, and feeling—the five senses. This is why God wrapped up Himself in the person of Jesus Christ and came and "dwelt among us." When the disciples wanted Jesus to show them what God is like, Jesus said, "He that hath seen me hath seen the Father." They saw Jesus relieving suffering, meeting financial needs, giving hope and new life to the downtrodden. They saw that Jesus is good, so they knew that God is good, for Jesus is God in action *(John 1:14; 14:7–10).*

God comes to us *through the Holy Spirit* so that there are no time and space barriers between God and us. God is everywhere…all the time.

So we don't think of three Gods when we say Father or Jesus Christ or Holy Spirit. We are talking about the ONE God who comes to us in ways and means which we can understand.

In 1 & 2 THESSALONIANS...
He Is Our Soon Coming King

JESUS MADE A promise. "I will come again" *(John 14:3)*. The Bible says, "There shall come in the last days scoffers...saying, Where is the promise of his coming?... But...the Lord is not slack concerning his promise... The day of the Lord WILL come" *(2 Peter 3:3–4,9–10)*.

Paul wrote to the Thessalonians, "The Lord himself shall descend from heaven with a shout, with the voice of the archangel, and with the trump of God: and the dead in Christ shall rise first: then we which are alive and remain shall be caught up together with them in the clouds, to meet the Lord in the air: and so shall we ever be with the Lord. Wherefore comfort one another with these words" *(1 Thessalonians 4:16–18)*.

The early Christians greeted each other with the word "Maranatha," which means *the Lord cometh*. These words comforted them when persecutions and trials came.

Some of the signs of Christ's coming are found in Matthew 16, 24, and 25; 1 Thessalonians 5:1–9;

2 Timothy 3:1–5; 4:3–4. Jesus, in anticipation of the troublesome events of the end time, had this to add by way of comfort to His redeemed people: "When these things begin to come to pass, then look up, and lift up your heads; for your redemption draweth nigh" *(Luke 21:28).*

So, we can live in love, courage, and calm certainty. We can plan our tomorrows with faith and yet live each day so that we can be prepared for the sudden appearance of our coming King. Maranatha! The Lord cometh!

In 1 & 2 TIMOTHY, He Is the Mediator Between God and Man

SINFUL MAN COULD NOT approach God without a mediator. Jesus Christ is the Mediator. "For there is one God, and one mediator between God and men, the man Christ Jesus" *(1 Timothy 2:5).*

Jesus came in to the world to bring about a reconciliation between God and man...to relieve the anger, intolerance, and alienation in all creation that came as a result of sin. On the cross, Jesus reached up with the right hand of His divine nature and took the hand of God; then with the left hand of His humanity, He reached down and took hold of the hand of man. He then pulled man up and God down. They were reconciled.

Even in our world of desperation, the marvel of Christ's reconciling power is still being experienced. Christ is the way to the heart of God. Jesus said, "Whatsoever ye shall ask the Father in my name, he will give it you" *(John 16:23)*.

Today, Jesus is at the right hand of God the Father making intercession for us *(Romans 8:34)*. We are encouraged to "come boldly unto the throne of grace" to find help in time of need *(Hebrews 4:16)*. Through Christ our Mediator, we can have access to all God's fullness in the *NOW.*

In TITUS...
He Is the Faithful Pastor

PAUL ADMONISHES TITUS regarding his pastoral duties and lays down the pattern for a faithful pastor to follow. He exhorts Titus to be an example himself of purity in conduct, in teaching and in speech: "For the grace of God that bringeth salvation hath appeared to all men, teaching us that, denying ungodliness and worldly lusts, we should live soberly, righteously, and godly, in this present world; looking for that blessed hope, and the glorious appearing of the great God and our Saviour Jesus Christ; who gave himself for us, that he might redeem us from all iniquity, and purify unto himself a peculiar people, zealous of good works. These things speak, and exhort, and rebuke with all authority" *(Titus 2:11–15)*.

Certainly Jesus Christ as the Faithful Pastor was our example. He said, "I have given you an example, that ye should do as I have done to you" *(John 13:15)*.

Jesus was a man whose words were positive, powerful, and full of authority. When He taught in the synagogue the people "were astonished at his doctrine: for he taught them as one that had authority, and not as the scribes" *(Mark 1:22)*.

At the heart of Christ's messages was, "Repent ye, and believe the gospel" *(Mark 1:15)*. He urged people to clean up their lives and separate themselves from evil. He was against sin because it destroys people. He said, "The thief [the devil] cometh not, but for to steal, and to kill, and to destroy: I am come that [you] might have life, and that [you] might have it more abundantly" *(John 10:10).*

In every way, Jesus Christ demonstrates the Faithful Pastor.

In PHILEMON...
He Is the Friend of the Oppressed

THE BOOK OF PHILEMON, the shortest of Paul's Epistles, reveals a wonderful expression of Christian love. It contains a tender and moving appeal in behalf of a runaway slave who had stolen money from his master, but who found the Lord Jesus Christ under Paul's ministry. Paul felt for the weakness of people. And no one was too insignificant for him to help. He was a friend to the oppressed. But the runaway found an even greater Friend in Jesus Christ. Paul promised to pay what the slave owed in money, but Jesus Christ had already paid his sin-debt.

Jesus said, "I have called you friends" *(John 15:15).* He also said, "I will never leave thee, nor forsake thee" *(Hebrews 13:5).* While there are friends in this world who stick by us, there are many friends who fail us in our hour of need. Jesus Christ is a Friend who "sticketh closer than a brother" *(Proverbs 18:24)*.

One of the deepest joys of the Christian life is our friendship with Jesus. He is a Friend who enters into all experiences of life with us. When the journey seems hard, Christ's love gives us strength. When disappointment comes, He comforts and encourages us. So close is this companionship with the Lord that it is possible to communicate with Him heart-to-heart. Not just with words that are detected by the human ear, but with those impulses of the Spirit that are felt by the inner man. Jesus is the eternally faithful Friend of the oppressed.

In HEBREWS...
He Is the Blood of the
Everlasting Covenant

THE CHILDREN OF ISRAEL had ordinances of commemoration and celebration, the chief of which was the Passover *(Exodus 12:23–27; 1 Peter 1:18–19)*.

The Passover (Lord's Supper) that Jesus had with His disciples on the night of His betrayal was the fulfillment of the memorial that had been instituted 1,600 years before. On that night Jesus introduced a new ordinance, which we know today as the Holy Communion. Jesus taught the Communion not as a mere ritual but as an integral part of our relationship with Him whereby our needs are met.

After the Passover supper had been eaten, "Jesus took bread. And when he had given thanks, he brake it, and said, Take, eat: this is my body, which is broken for you... This cup is the new testament in my blood: this do ye, as oft as ye drink it, in remembrance of me" *(1 Corinthians 11:23–30)*.

The bread and the wine are not what the Communion is all about. They are but emblems of the Man Jesus...points of contact to reach Him. The Communion is a meaningful act of faith through which you can allow the Holy Spirit to bring to your remembrance the wonderful life and works of Jesus so that you can relate to Him as a Person and take His sweetness into your spirit.

The Communion is to strengthen you. How weak we can be sometimes wanting to throw up our hands and say life is so hard. But as you by faith receive an infusion of His life and Spirit throughout your being…you can receive nourishing, strengthening, and healing for your entire life.

You can take the Communion when your problems are the worst, and your needs are the most severe. Just those few moments in which you eat the bread and drink the cup—remembering Jesus as the Source of your life, and grasping the meaning of His harmonious, whole body for your life—can cause you to look at your needs in an entirely different way.

Your problems don't need to get you down, because through the power of the Communion you can have an opportunity to reach out to God, your Source, who can help you make progress through that problem. Jesus can come alive to you in a new dimension. And through Christ, the blood of the everlasting covenant, a complete wholeness and harmony can begin in your life (*Hebrews 13:20–21*).

In JAMES…
He Is the Lord Who Raiseth the Sick

"IS ANY SICK among you? let him call for the elders of the church; and let them pray over him, anointing him with oil in the name of the Lord: and the prayer of faith shall save the sick, and the Lord shall raise him up; and if he have committed sins, they shall be forgiven" *(James 5:14–15)*.

Healing for the whole man—body, mind, and spirit—is one of the provisions of the Atonement. While on earth, Christ spent two-thirds of His time healing people. Today, He still looks upon sickness as something to be healed—not endured. Healing and continual health are designed to be ours by divine right.

James 5:16 goes on to say, "Confess your faults one to another, and pray one for another, that YE may be healed."

Pray one for another is possibly one of the most important things that you and I can learn for our healing. Often when I pray for someone, I suggest a "two-way prayer." In other words, I ask the other person to pray for me first before I begin my prayer for him. This is to help the sick person open up to a miracle by planting a seed of concern for someone else first.

The Lord is saying to us, "You pray for someone else so that YOU may also be healed. Put the seed in first, so that I can have something from your heart to work with."

This is another way of saying, "Give, and it shall be given unto you" *(Luke 6:38)*—another way of seeding for a miracle. Giving is important. However, for it to be a seed of faith, it has to be a by-product of an obedient heart...one that is opening up. Thus, you can open yourself up to God, to others, and to miracles of healing for every area of your life.

In 1 & 2 PETER...
He Is the Chief Shepherd
Who Soon Shall Appear

JESUS CHRIST LIKENED himself to a shepherd. He loved and cared for His "sheep" while on earth—even died for them—and appointed under-shepherds to work under Him and continue His work.

Three times Christ asked Peter, "Lovest thou me?" Each time Peter replied, "Yea, Lord; thou knowest that I love thee." With each affirmation, Jesus said unto him, "Feed my sheep" *(John 21:15–17)*.

This same charge has been passed down to other faithful shepherds whom the Lord has seen fit to entrust with His sheep.

"Feed the flock of God which is among you... not by constraint, but willingly; not for filthy lucre, but of a ready mind; neither as being lords over God's heritage, but being ensamples to the flock." This charge holds a great promise: "And when the chief Shepherd shall appear, ye shall receive a crown of glory that fadeth not away" *(1 Peter 5:2–4)*.

In 1 & 2 & 3 JOHN...
He Is Love

THE GREATEST THING God ever showed me...the greatest thing I know today...is that God is a good God. And He loves us.

I discovered this truth one morning as I was rushing to make an early class at a university I was attending while I pastored a church. I had resolved that each morning I would read something from the Bible. In my rush that day I simply opened the Bible at random to read, and it fell open to 3 John 2—God's number one wish for us: "Beloved, I wish above all things that thou mayest prosper and be in health, even as thy soul prospereth." I could scarcely believe my eyes. This verse was simply beautiful. Yet it had something more than beauty. It had power and it gripped my heart. For it was saying, *God is a good God!*

I saw too many people who accepted life's tragedies as God's will, and they didn't expect Him to change the inequalities of life. One was to be sick...another well. One poor...another rich. One happy...another miserable. And that was that. Religion was not divine deliverance but acceptance of life's inadequacies. But something inside me said this wasn't true.

This Scripture is just as real to me now as it was then. It means God is a good God and the devil is a bad devil. There is no badness in God and no goodness in the devil. The good things come from God and the bad things come from the devil.

It is a simple but powerful truth that it is difficult to believe God to bless you when at the same time you believe He is cursing you. It is difficult to believe His promise to supply all your needs if you believe He wants you to be poor. And how can you have faith for God to heal you when you believe He has afflicted your body?

Notice the first word of God's divine wish. *Beloved.* That's a word you reserve for somebody who is dear and close to you. And it's the way God feels about you. As His beloved, it's as if your name is written in the Scriptures. Try it. *I, _____, am beloved of God. And God wishes for me to prosper and be in health, even as my soul prospers.*

In JUDE...
He Is the Lord Coming with
Ten Thousands of His Saints

JUDE SAID, "BEHOLD, the Lord cometh with ten thousands of his saints" *(Jude 14).*

There is a spiritual awakening stirring in the world, and a dominant note is the strong awareness that Jesus is soon coming again.

It isn't too unusual these days to see a car drive by with the slogans, **Jesus Is Coming Soon** and **Any Day Now**, painted all over it.

At Christ's Ascension the angels who stood by proclaimed, "This same Jesus, which is taken up from you into heaven, shall so come in like manner as ye have seen him go into heaven" *(Acts 1:11).*

The signs we see today fulfilling prophecies concerning Christ's second coming are astounding, giving new hope that surely "it is nigh, even at the doors" *(Mark 13:29).*

In REVELATION...
He Is Our King of Kings
and Lord of Lords!

"AND HE HATH on his vesture and on his thigh a name written, KING OF KINGS, AND LORD OF LORDS" *(Revelation 19:16).*

Christ's first coming was one of humility. He was born in a lowly manger. Before He died He was spit upon and mocked with a crown of thorns and a scarlet robe. JESUS OF NAZARETH THE KING OF THE JEWS was the inscription on the cross above His head. This, too, was to humiliate and ridicule Christ. His crucifiers did not understand that He came not to establish a literal kingdom, but a spiritual kingdom in the hearts of men.

Christ's second coming to the earth will be a triumphant one as King of kings and Lord of lords. This time, He is coming to triumph over His enemies. "The Lord shall be king over all the earth" *(Zechariah 14:9)*. His true name will be written on His vesture and on His thigh: KING OF KINGS, AND LORD OF LORDS. On His head will be "many crowns." At last it will be true that "the Lord God omnipotent reigneth." Christ's rule will be one of peace.

People will realize His kingship and lordship, for "God also hath highly exalted him, and given him a name which is above every name: that at the name of Jesus every knee should bow, of things in heaven, and things in earth, and things under the earth; and that every tongue should confess that Jesus Christ is Lord, to the glory of God the Father" *(Philippians 2:9–11).*

Jesus Christ Is...

Jesus Christ is...
> Abel's Sacrifice, Noah's Rainbow,
> Abraham's Lamb, Isaac's Well,
> Jacob's Ladder, Ezekiel's Burden,
> Judah's Scepter, Moses' Rod,
> David's Slingshot, Hezekiah's Sundial.

Jesus Christ is...
> a Husband to the Widow,
> a Father to the Orphan.

To those traveling in the dark night,
> He is the Bright and Morning Star.

To those in the lonesome valley,
> He is the Lily of the Valley,
> the Rose of Sharon,
> Honey in the Rock, and
> the Staff of Life.

He is the Pearl of Great Price.

He is the Rock in a Weary Land.

He is the Counselor.

He is the Everlasting Father,
> and the government of our lives
> is on His shoulders.

He is Peter's Shadow and
   John's Pearly White City.
He is Jesus…Jesus of Nazareth,
   Son of the Living God!